# Study Guide

# Student Workbook for

# Al Capone Does My Shirts

## By: John Pennington

The Quick Student Workbooks are designed to get students thinking critically about the text they read and providing a guided study format to facilitate in improved learning and retention. Teachers and Homeschool Instructors may use them to improve student learning and organization.

Students will construct and identify the following areas of knowledge.

Character Identification

Events

Location

Vocabulary

Main Idea

Conflict

And more as appropriate to the text.

This is a workbook for students to determine the above areas. This is not a study guide, cliff notes, or Teacher's guide.

How to use this workbook

1. Complete as many entries as possible for each chapter.

2. Not all spaces need to be filled, move on when you have exhausted the information for the chapter.

3. Complete the Review page at the end to bring the information together.

4. Notes Pages are located after the Chapter Pages. Use them to record any information not covered in the Chapter Pages.

5. Notes on the author can be kept on pages 4 and 5.

Need a Teachers Guide created?

Upgrade to the Lessons on Demand line of books!

Send requests and questions to Johndavidpennington@yahoo.com

## Author Notes

## Before Reading Questions

What is the reason for reading this book?

What do you already know about this book?

What, based on the cover, do you think this book is about?

## Before Reading Questions

Have you read any other books by this author?

Is this book part of a series? If so what are the other books?

What are you looking forward to when reading this book?

* After Reading questions can be found in the back.

NAME:

TEACHER:

Date:

### Chapter

### Events

1.

2.

3.

4.

5.

\* <u>Not all number lines will have answers.</u>

### Possible Future Events

1.

2.

### Characters

1.

2.

3.

4.

5.

6.

### Key Terms / Vocabulary

1.

2.

3.

4.

### Locations

1.

2.

### Conflicts / Problems

1.

2.

3.

4.

### Main Idea

NAME:

TEACHER:

Date:

Chapter

* Not all number lines will have answers.

Characters
1.
2.
3.
4.
5.
6.

Locations
1.
2.

Conflicts / Problems
1.
2.
3.
4.

Events
1.
2.
3.
4.
5.

Possible Future Events
1.
2.

Key Terms / Vocabulary
1.
2.
3.
4.

Main Idea

NAME:

TEACHER:

Date:

## Chapter

* Not all number lines will have answers.

## Characters

1.
2.
3.
4.
5.
6.

## Locations

1.
2.

## Conflicts / Problems

1.
2.
3.
4.

## Events

1.
2.
3.
4.
5.

## Possible Future Events

1.
2.

## Key Terms / Vocabulary

1.
2.
3.
4.

## Main Idea

NAME:

TEACHER:

Date:

## Chapter

\* <u>Not all number lines will have answers.</u>

## Characters

1.
2.
3.
4.
5.
6.

## Locations

1.
2.

## Conflicts / Problems

1.
2.
3.
4.

## Events

1.
2.
3.
4.
5.

## Possible Future Events

1.
2.

## Key Terms / Vocabulary

1.
2.
3.
4.

## Main Idea

NAME:

TEACHER:

Date:

### Chapter

### Events

1.

2.

3.

4.

5.

* <u>Not all number lines will have answers.</u>

### Characters

1.

2.

3.

4.

5.

6.

### Possible Future Events

1.

2.

### Key Terms / Vocabulary

1.

2.

3.

4.

### Locations

1.

2.

### Conflicts / Problems

1.

2.

3.

4.

### Main Idea

NAME:

TEACHER:

Date:

**Chapter**

**Events**

1.

2.

3.

4.

5.

* <u>Not all number lines will have answers.</u>

**Characters**

1.

2.

3.

4.

5.

6.

**Possible Future Events**

1.

2.

**Key Terms / Vocabulary**

1.

2.

3.

4.

**Locations**

1.

2.

**Conflicts / Problems**

1.

2.

3.

4.

**Main Idea**

**NAME:**

**TEACHER:**

**Date:**

**Chapter**

* <u>Not all number lines will have answers.</u>

**Characters**

1.
2.
3.
4.
5.
6.

**Locations**

1.
2.

**Conflicts / Problems**

1.
2.
3.
4.

**Events**

1.
2.
3.
4.
5.

**Possible Future Events**

1.
2.

**Key Terms / Vocabulary**

1.
2.
3.
4.

**Main Idea**

NAME:

TEACHER:

Date:

## Chapter

\* <u>Not all number lines will have answers.</u>

## Characters

1.
2.
3.
4.
5.
6.

## Locations

1.
2.

## Conflicts / Problems

1.
2.
3.
4.

## Events

1.
2.
3.
4.
5.

## Possible Future Events

1.
2.

## Key Terms / Vocabulary

1.
2.
3.
4.

## Main Idea

NAME:

TEACHER:

Date:

## Chapter

* Not all number lines will have answers.

## Characters

1.

2.

3.

4.

5.

6.

## Locations

1.

2.

## Conflicts / Problems

1.

2.

3.

4.

## Events

1.

2.

3.

4.

5.

## Possible Future Events

1.

2.

## Key Terms / Vocabulary

1.

2.

3.

4.

## Main Idea

NAME:

TEACHER:

Date:

Chapter

Events
1.
2.
3.
4.
5.

* Not all number lines will have answers.

Characters
1.
2.
3.
4.
5.
6.

Possible Future Events
1.
2.

Key Terms / Vocabulary
1.
2.
3.
4.

Locations
1.
2.

Conflicts / Problems
1.
2.
3.
4.

Main Idea

NAME:

TEACHER:

Date:

## Chapter

*Not all number lines will have answers.*

## Characters

1.
2.
3.
4.
5.
6.

## Locations

1.
2.

## Conflicts / Problems

1.
2.
3.
4.

## Events

1.
2.
3.
4.
5.

## Possible Future Events

1.
2.

## Key Terms / Vocabulary

1.
2.
3.
4.

## Main Idea

NAME:

TEACHER:

Date:

## Chapter

\* <u>Not all number lines will have answers.</u>

## Characters

1.

2.

3.

4.

5.

6.

## Locations

1.

2.

## Conflicts / Problems

1.

2.

3.

4.

## Events

1.

2.

3.

4.

5.

## Possible Future Events

1.

2.

## Key Terms / Vocabulary

1.

2.

3.

4.

## Main Idea

NAME:

TEACHER:

Date:

## Chapter

* Not all number lines will have answers.

## Characters

1.

2.

3.

4.

5.

6.

## Locations

1.

2.

## Conflicts / Problems

1.

2.

3.

4.

## Events

1.

2.

3.

4.

5.

## Possible Future Events

1.

2.

## Key Terms / Vocabulary

1.

2.

3.

4.

## Main Idea

NAME:

TEACHER:

Date:

## Chapter

\* <u>Not all number lines will have answers.</u>

## Characters

1.

2.

3.

4.

5.

6.

## Locations

1.

2.

## Conflicts / Problems

1.

2.

3.

4.

## Events

1.

2.

3.

4.

5.

## Possible Future Events

1.

2.

## Key Terms / Vocabulary

1.

2.

3.

4.

## Main Idea

NAME:

TEACHER:

Date:

Chapter

Events

1.

2.

3.

4.

5.

* Not all number lines will have answers.

Characters

1.

2.

3.

4.

5.

6.

Possible Future Events

1.

2.

Key Terms / Vocabulary

1.

2.

3.

4.

Locations

1.

2.

Conflicts / Problems

1.

2.

3.

4.

Main Idea

NAME:

TEACHER:

Date:

## Chapter

\* <u>Not all number lines will have answers.</u>

## Characters

1.
2.
3.
4.
5.
6.

## Locations

1.
2.

## Conflicts / Problems

1.
2.
3.
4.

## Events

1.
2.
3.
4.
5.

## Possible Future Events

1.
2.

## Key Terms / Vocabulary

1.
2.
3.
4.

## Main Idea

NAME:

TEACHER:

Date:

**Chapter**

* <u>Not all number lines will have answers.</u>

**Characters**

1.
2.
3.
4.
5.
6.

**Locations**

1.
2.

**Conflicts / Problems**

1.
2.
3.
4.

**Events**

1.
2.
3.
4.
5.

**Possible Future Events**

1.
2.

**Key Terms / Vocabulary**

1.
2.
3.
4.

**Main Idea**

NAME:

TEACHER:

Date:

Chapter

Events
1.
2.
3.
4.
5.

* Not all number lines will have answers.

Possible Future Events
1.
2.

Characters
1.
2.
3.
4.
5.
6.

Key Terms / Vocabulary
1.
2.
3.
4.

Locations
1.
2.

Conflicts / Problems
1.
2.
3.
4.

Main Idea

NAME:

TEACHER:

Date:

**Chapter**

**Events**

1.
2.
3.
4.
5.

\* <u>Not all number lines will have answers.</u>

**Characters**

1.
2.
3.
4.
5.
6.

**Possible Future Events**

1.
2.

**Key Terms / Vocabulary**

1.
2.
3.
4.

**Locations**

1.
2.

**Conflicts / Problems**

1.
2.
3.
4.

**Main Idea**

NAME:

TEACHER:

Date:

**Chapter**

**Events**

1.

2.

3.

4.

5.

\* <u>Not all number lines will have answers.</u>

**Characters**

1.

2.

3.

4.

5.

6.

**Possible Future Events**

1.

2.

**Key Terms / Vocabulary**

1.

2.

3.

4.

**Locations**

1.

2.

**Conflicts / Problems**

1.

2.

3.

4.

**Main Idea**

NAME:

TEACHER:

Date:

## Chapter

* <u>Not all number lines will have answers.</u>

## Characters
1.
2.
3.
4.
5.
6.

## Locations
1.
2.

## Conflicts / Problems
1.
2.
3.
4.

## Events
1.
2.
3.
4.
5.

## Possible Future Events
1.
2.

## Key Terms / Vocabulary
1.
2.
3.
4.

## Main Idea

NAME:

TEACHER:

Date:

Chapter

\* <u>Not all number lines will have answers.</u>

Characters

1.

2.

3.

4.

5.

6.

Locations

1.

2.

Conflicts / Problems

1.

2.

3.

4.

Events

1.

2.

3.

4.

5.

Possible Future Events

1.

2.

Key Terms / Vocabulary

1.

2.

3.

4.

Main Idea

NAME:

TEACHER:

Date:

## Chapter

\* <u>Not all number lines will have answers.</u>

## Characters

1.
2.
3.
4.
5.
6.

## Locations

1.
2.

## Conflicts / Problems

1.
2.
3.
4.

## Events

1.
2.
3.
4.
5.

## Possible Future Events

1.
2.

## Key Terms / Vocabulary

1.
2.
3.
4.

## Main Idea

NAME:

TEACHER:

Date:

Chapter

* Not all number lines will have answers.

Events

1.

2.

3.

4.

5.

Characters

1.

2.

3.

4.

5.

6.

Possible Future Events

1.

2.

Locations

1.

2.

Key Terms / Vocabulary

1.

2.

3.

4.

Conflicts / Problems

1.

2.

3.

4.

Main Idea

NAME:

TEACHER:

Date:

## Chapter

* <u>Not all number lines will have answers.</u>

## Characters

1.

2.

3.

4.

5.

6.

## Locations

1.

2.

## Conflicts / Problems

1.

2.

3.

4.

## Events

1.

2.

3.

4.

5.

## Possible Future Events

1.

2.

## Key Terms / Vocabulary

1.

2.

3.

4.

## Main Idea

NAME:

TEACHER:

Date:

### Chapter

\* <u>Not all number lines will have answers.</u>

### Characters

1.

2.

3.

4.

5.

6.

### Locations

1.

2.

### Conflicts / Problems

1.

2.

3.

4.

### Events

1.

2.

3.

4.

5.

### Possible Future Events

1.

2.

### Key Terms / Vocabulary

1.

2.

3.

4.

### Main Idea

NAME:

TEACHER:

Date:

## Chapter

* <u>Not all number lines will have answers.</u>

## Characters

1.
2.
3.
4.
5.
6.

## Locations

1.
2.

## Conflicts / Problems

1.
2.
3.
4.

## Events

1.
2.
3.
4.
5.

## Possible Future Events

1.
2.

## Key Terms / Vocabulary

1.
2.
3.
4.

## Main Idea

NAME:

TEACHER:

Date:

Chapter

* Not all number lines will have answers.

Characters
1.
2.
3.
4.
5.
6.

Locations
1.
2.

Conflicts / Problems
1.
2.
3.
4.

Events
1.
2.
3.
4.
5.

Possible Future Events
1.
2.

Key Terms / Vocabulary
1.
2.
3.
4.

Main Idea

NAME:

TEACHER:

Date:

**Chapter**

**Events**

1.

2.

3.

4.

5.

\* <u>Not all number lines will have answers.</u>

**Characters**

1.

2.

3.

4.

5.

6.

**Possible Future Events**

1.

2.

**Key Terms / Vocabulary**

1.

2.

3.

4.

**Locations**

1.

2.

**Conflicts / Problems**

1.

2.

3.

4.

**Main Idea**

NAME:

TEACHER:

Date:

## Chapter

* Not all number lines will have answers.

## Characters
1.
2.
3.
4.
5.
6.

## Locations
1.
2.

## Conflicts / Problems
1.
2.
3.
4.

## Events
1.
2.
3.
4.
5.

## Possible Future Events
1.
2.

## Key Terms / Vocabulary
1.
2.
3.
4.

## Main Idea

NAME:

TEACHER:

Date:

## Chapter

\* <u>Not all number lines will have answers.</u>

## Characters

1.

2.

3.

4.

5.

6.

## Locations

1.

2.

## Conflicts / Problems

1.

2.

3.

4.

## Events

1.

2.

3.

4.

5.

## Possible Future Events

1.

2.

## Key Terms / Vocabulary

1.

2.

3.

4.

## Main Idea

NAME:

TEACHER:

Date:

## Chapter

\* <u>Not all number lines will have answers.</u>

## Characters

1.

2.

3.

4.

5.

6.

## Locations

1.

2.

## Conflicts / Problems

1.

2.

3.

4.

## Events

1.

2.

3.

4.

5.

## Possible Future Events

1.

2.

## Key Terms / Vocabulary

1.

2.

3.

4.

## Main Idea

NAME:

TEACHER:

Date:

## Chapter

* Not all number lines will have answers.

## Events

1.

2.

3.

4.

5.

## Characters

1.

2.

3.

4.

5.

6.

## Possible Future Events

1.

2.

## Key Terms / Vocabulary

1.

2.

3.

4.

## Locations

1.

2.

## Conflicts / Problems

1.

2.

3.

4.

## Main Idea

NAME:

TEACHER:

Date:

Chapter

* Not all number lines will have answers.

Characters

1.

2.

3.

4.

5.

6.

Locations

1.

2.

Conflicts / Problems

1.

2.

3.

4.

Events

1.

2.

3.

4.

5.

Possible Future Events

1.

2.

Key Terms / Vocabulary

1.

2.

3.

4.

Main Idea

NAME:

TEACHER:

Date:

## Chapter

## Events

1.
2.
3.
4.
5.

* <u>Not all number lines will have answers.</u>

## Characters

1.
2.
3.
4.
5.
6.

## Possible Future Events

1.
2.

## Key Terms / Vocabulary

1.
2.
3.
4.

## Locations

1.
2.

## Conflicts / Problems

1.
2.
3.
4.

## Main Idea

**NAME:**

**TEACHER:**

**Date:**

## Chapter

* Not all number lines will have answers.

## Characters

1.
2.
3.
4.
5.
6.

## Locations

1.
2.

## Conflicts / Problems

1.
2.
3.
4.

## Events

1.
2.
3.
4.
5.

## Possible Future Events

1.
2.

## Key Terms / Vocabulary

1.
2.
3.
4.

## Main Idea

NAME:

TEACHER:

Date:

## Chapter

* Not all number lines will have answers.

## Characters

1.
2.
3.
4.
5.
6.

## Locations

1.
2.

## Conflicts / Problems

1.
2.
3.
4.

## Events

1.
2.
3.
4.
5.

## Possible Future Events

1.
2.

## Key Terms / Vocabulary

1.
2.
3.
4.

## Main Idea

NAME:

TEACHER:

Date:

**Chapter**

**Events**

1.
2.
3.
4.
5.

\* Not all number lines will have answers.

**Characters**

1.
2.
3.
4.
5.
6.

**Possible Future Events**

1.
2.

**Key Terms / Vocabulary**

1.
2.
3.
4.

**Locations**

1.
2.

**Conflicts / Problems**

1.
2.
3.
4.

**Main Idea**

NAME:

TEACHER:

Date:

**Chapter**

**Events**

1.

2.

3.

4.

5.

* <u>Not all number lines will have answers.</u>

**Characters**

1.

2.

3.

4.

5.

6.

**Possible Future Events**

1.

2.

**Key Terms / Vocabulary**

1.

2.

3.

4.

**Locations**

1.

2.

**Conflicts / Problems**

1.

2.

3.

4.

**Main Idea**

NAME:

TEACHER:

Date:

### Chapter

### Events

1.

2.

3.

4.

5.

\* Not all number lines will have answers.

### Characters

1.

2.

3.

4.

5.

6.

### Possible Future Events

1.

2.

### Key Terms / Vocabulary

1.

2.

3.

4.

### Locations

1.

2.

### Conflicts / Problems

1.

2.

3.

4.

### Main Idea

What parts of the book were the most enjoyable?

Which characters were your favorite and why?

Write a summary of the book.

What are the 5 most important events?

Write a review of the book.

What is likely to be a plot to the next book?

Draw an advertisement for the book

# Character Sketch

## Name

## Personality/ Distinguishing marks

## Draw a picture

## Connections to other characters

## Important Actions

## Character Sketch

### Name

### Personality/ Distinguishing marks

### Draw a picture

### Connections to other characters

### Important Actions

# Character Sketch

## Name

## Personality/ Distinguishing marks

## Draw a picture

## Connections to other characters

## Important Actions

## Character Sketch

### Name

### Personality/ Distinguishing marks

### Draw a picture

### Connections to other characters

### Important Actions

## Character Sketch

### Name

### Personality/ Distinguishing marks

### Draw a picture

### Connections to other characters

### Important Actions

# Compare and Contrast

## Venn Diagram

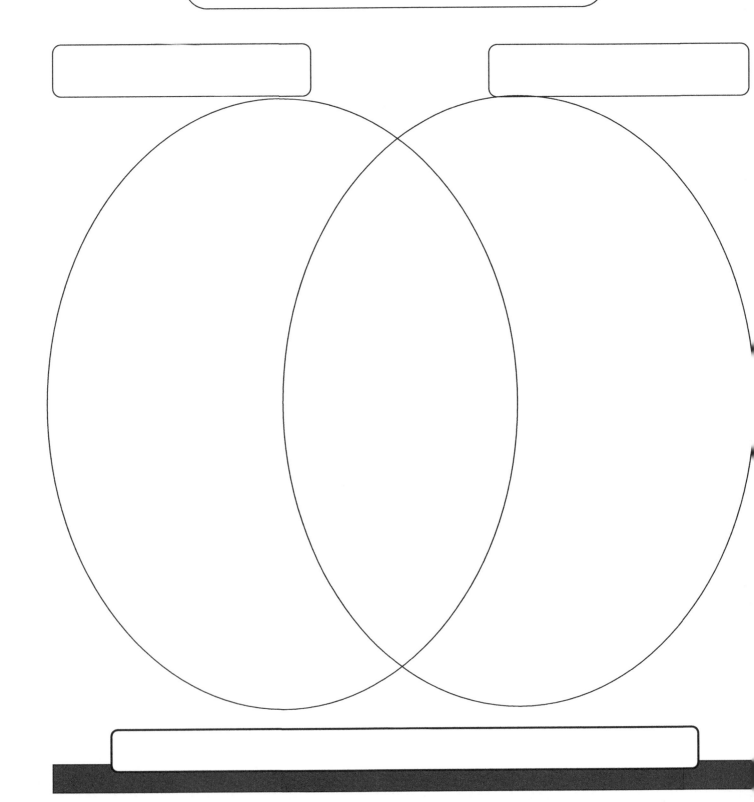

Notes

Notes

## Notes

NAME:

TEACHER:

Date:

* <u>Not all number lines will have</u>
<u>answers.</u>

## Main Characters

1.

2.

3.

4.

5.

6.

7.

8.

9.

10.

11.

12.

13.

14.

15.

16.

17.

18.

## Important Locations

1.

2.

3.

4.

5.

## Resolved Conflicts / Problems

1.

2.

3.

4.

5.

6.

7.

8.

9.

10.

11.

12.

NAME:

TEACHER:

Continued

Date:

## Most Important Events

1.
2.
3.
4.
5.
6.
7.
8.
9.
10.

## Main Idea of the Novel

## Unresolved Conflicts / Problems

1.
2.
3.
4.
5.
6.
7.
8.
9.
10.
11.
12.

## Possible Future Events

1.
2.
3.
4.
5.
6.

Made in the USA
Coppell, TX
30 January 2022

72694115R00037